"Potjie"
For two

Roelof Beukes

DEDICATION

To my mentor/publisher/editor/translator/best friend and many other titles…without you another book would not be possible, thank you for pushing my limits.

CONTENTS

Roelof Beukes

ACKNOWLEDGMENTS

Thank you Oom Frikkie and Tannie Ina for introducing me to this modern way of potjiekos.

THE POTJIE

After months of searching for the right dish to use for an intimate date to rekindle the old flame, I one day was introduced by friends of ours to an old South-African favored in a new way and ever since then I found myself constantly looking at ways to make it more fun for the two of us.

The preparation behind and even the making of the pot or "potjie" leads to conversations and with a glass wine the laughter can flow quick.

In my view Potjiekos for two is nothing other than the south African version of fondue but there are more to it than just a fondue. Potjiekos" Pronounced "poi-key" (pot) and "poi-key-cos" (pot food). In South Africa this means only one thing, food prepared outdoors in a cast iron, round, three legged pot using either wood coals or charcoal. Today, cooking up a "potjie" has evolved into a unique social happening, a tradition almost as popular as the legendary "Braai" (barbecue).

The reason I chosen this unique dish for a special date with your loved one or as the perfect dish for camping is solely because of Potjiekos ability to become one's own. Yes no matter how you furrow you prepare this dish by recipe at some stage you will add or remove or multiply an ingredient

The "Potjie" is not something I just thought of in a moment of desperation to rekindle the passion for the cold winter nights.O no Long before the arrival of the early settlers in the Cape, the Bantu people who were migrating into South Africa, learned the use of the cast iron cooking pot from Arab traders and later the Portuguese colonists. When the first Dutch settlers arrived in the Cape, they to brought with them their ways of cooking food in heavy cast iron pots, which hung from the kitchen hearth above the fire.

The round potbellied cast iron pot was the perfect cooking utensil to suit the nomadic lifestyle of the Voortrekkers (pioneers) during the 17th and 18th centuries. "Potjiekos" evolving as a stew made of venison and vegetables (if available), cooked in the potjie. As trekkers shot wild game, it was added to the pot. The large bones were included to thicken the stew. Each day when the wagons stopped, the pot was placed over a fire to simmer. New bones replaced old and fresh meat replaced meat eaten. Game included venison, poultry such as guinea fowl, wart hog, bushpig, rabbit and hare. The pot with its contents protected by a layer of fat was hooked under the wagon by the Voortrekkers while traveling and unhooked at the next stop to be put on the fire again.

The range of different recipes is as wide as the imagination stretches and preparing a potjie meal is very much an individual thing. The best meat to use for "potjiekos" is what is known as stewing beef, sinewy and gelatinous cuts of beef which become deliciously tender when simmered for a long time, developing a strong meaty flavor. Other meat such as venison, mutton, chicken and even fish make ideal "potjies".

As much as the stew are important so are the side serving which is always either rice, barely or even samp. You will find I chosen 5 starters and 5 deserts for your evening or picnic or camp night to complimant the potjie but very important : **Although much preparation went in to the quantities always picture this author as a fat guy who loves food and use your own desecration in some circumstances.**

When choosing your potjie, first consider the size. For a family of four to six a size 3 pot will do but because we doing this traditional dish in a modern way we using a ¼ size pot for the stew part and for the side dish we using a ½ size pot . As a rule of thumb calculate about ½ liter per person if you are serving it with rice or similar cooked separately. If you are serving just Potjie kos calculate about ½ liter per person. Make sure it has no cracks and very important ensure that the lid seals properly.

Before cooking your meal for the first time, you need to prepare your pot to get rid of any black deposit or iron taste.

Step 1, scour the inside of the pot with using sandpaper, wash and grease both the inside and outside with fat.

Step 2, Fill the pot with leftover vegetables or peels and cook over a slow fire for a few hours, repeat this process a few times.

Step 3, now prepare your potjie for storage, rinse the pot with warm soapy water and then coat the inside with a thin layer of fat or cooking oil to prevent rusting, do this after every meal.

Ps. The more frequent the usage the smoother and shinier it will become.

The fire is an crucial part of creating a culinary "potjie" masterpiece. Unlike a "braai", the choice of wood or charcoal does not make much difference, as long as you can regulate the heat. Most experts recommend hardwood or good quality charcoal. For rainy days, you could also use a gas fire, the gas flame is more easily regulated and because of this element in the dish and the rain factor. I made my own versatile potjie stove. Now the "potjie" stove is basically a small wooden box with a lid on tiled on the one side to serve as a cutting bord and on the other side it has a hole in the middle for where the cooking gel in a small stainless-steel container comes but you can also use a normal fire or even mini fires if you have aluminum foil pans. I just found a little bit effort in making a "potjie" stove will get you a lot more brownie points by your guest or partner.

You will find the liquid gel tents to burn for at least 3 hours more than ample time needed for your pot and with this said I need to remind you to also keep in mind to start long before your dinner time, because you need to keep in mind not only your cooking time, but also the time it takes for your pot to heat up which does takes about 15 minutes. Remember it is all part of the plan as it allows for time to get to know each other, and if you're a smooth operator work some dancing in the moonlight.

Potjie is all about preparation and I found cutting things up and neatly don't just leave a good impression but it also are making life easy during actual cooking. Mainly because arranging the food in layers is the other important part. The meat usually comes first. Add a dash of cooking oil or some fat in the pot, add meat the meat and brown thoroughly. This is essential to improve the appearance of the meat. Add sliced onions, garlic and spice and stir the meat to seal in the flavor. Cook the meat till nearly done.

Now pack in the layers of vegetables in order of their cooking times, like carrots and potatoes first and thereafter sweet potatoes, pumpkin, mushrooms etc. Arrange the vegetables in layers around the sides, if adding rice to potjie, form a hollow in the middle for the rice. Add liquid / marinade until about 2 cm under the top layer of vegetables and just leave it for a couple of hours until ready. Replace the lid and do not stir again. Add a little liquid when the food tends to cook dry, but only a little at a time as watery "potjie" is not nice and too much flavor is lost.

When ready, stir once to ensure an even mix of meat and vegetables, dish up and enjoy a memorable meal.

REMEMBER ONE ¼ SIZE POTJIE SERVES ONLY ONE PERSON AND FOR THE RICE ONE ½ SIZE POTJIE WILL SERVE MORE THAN ENOUGH RICE FOR TWO.

CONVERSION

I decided to add this section mainly because I hate it when they talk about ounces in a recipe book and I only know grams and kilograms.

U.S. to Metric	Metric to U.S.	Metric to Imperial
Liquid	**Liquid**	**Liquid**
1 tsp. = 4.929 mL	1 mL = 0.033814 fl. oz.	30ml = 1 oz
1 Tbls. = 14.787 mL	1 mL = 0.061024 cu. in.	60ml = 2 oz
1 fl. Dr. = 3.6967 mL	1 mL = 0.2029 tsp.	100ml = 3 oz
1 fl. Oz. = 29.57353 mL	1 mL = 0.0676 Tbls.	125ml = 4 oz
1 cup = 236.59 mL	1 dl = 3.3814 fl. oz.	150ml = 5 oz (¼ pint)
1 cup = 2.366 dl	1 dl = 6.1024 cu. in.	190ml = 6 oz
1 cup = 0.2366 l	1 dl = 20.29 tsp.	250ml = 8 oz
1 gi. = 118.294 mL	1 dl = 6.76 Tbls.	300ml = 10 oz (½ pint)
1 gi. = 1.18294 dl	1 dl = 27.05 fl. dr.	500ml = 16 oz
1 gi. = 0.118294 l	1 dl = 0.423 cups	600ml = 20 oz (1pint)
1 pt. = 473.1765 mL	1 dl = 0.845 gi.	1000ml (1 litre) = 1¾ pints
1 pt. = 4.731765 dl	1 dl = 0.21134 pt.	**Dry**
1 pt. = 0.4731765 l	1 dl = 0.10567 qt.	15g = ½oz
1 qt. =9.4635 dl	1 l =33.814 fl. oz.	30g = 1oz
1 qt. = 0.94635 l	1 l = 61.024 cu. in.	60g = 2oz
1 gal. = 37.854 dl	1 l = 67.6 Tbls.	90g = 3oz
1 gal. = 3.7854 l	1 l = 270.5 fl. dr.	125g = 4oz (¼lb)
1 firkin = 34.069 l	1 l = 4.23 cups	155g = 5oz
1 hhd = 238.48 l	1 l = 8.45 gi.	185g = 6oz
Dry	1 l = 2.1134 pt.	220g = 7oz
1 pt. = 0.551 l	1 l = 1.0567 qt.	250g = 8oz (½lb)
1 qt. = 1.101 l	1 l = 0.26417 gal.	280g = 9oz
1 pk. = 8.81 l	1 l = 0.029353 firkins	315g = 10oz
1 bu. = 35.25 l	**Dry**	345g = 11oz
Weight	1 l = 1.8162 pt.	375g = 12oz (¾lb)
1 oz. = 28.35 g	1 l = 0.9081 qt.	410g = 13oz
1 lb. = 453.59 g	**Weight**	440g = 14oz
1 lb. = 0.454 kg	1 g = 0.035274 oz.	470g = 15oz
	1 g = 0.0022046 lb.	500g = 16oz (1lb)
	1 kg = 35.274 oz.	750g = 24oz (1½lb)
	1 kg = 2.2046 lb.	1kg = 32oz (2lb)

Equivalent Measures		Volume Equivalents	
3 teaspoons	= 1 tablespoon	1/4 teaspoon = 1 ml	
½ tablespoon	= 1-1/2 teaspoons	½ teaspoon = 2 ml	
2 tablespoons	= 1 fluid ounce	1 teaspoon = 5 ml	
4 tablespoons	= 1/4 cup	1 tablespoon = 15 ml	
5-1/3 tablespoons	= 1/3 cup	1/4 cup = 65 ml	
8 tablespoons	= ½ cup	1 cup = 250 ml	
10-2/3 tablespoons	= 2/3 cup		
12 tablespoons	= 3/4 cup		
16 tablespoons	= 1 cup		
6 tablespoons	= 8 fluid ounces		
1/8 cup	= 2 tablespoons		
1/4 cup	= 4 tablespoons		
1/4 cup	= 2 fluid ounces		
1/3 cup	= 5 tablespoons plus 1 teaspoon		
½ cup = 8 tablespoons			
1 cup = 16 tablespoons			
1 cup = 8 fluid ounces			
1 cup = ½ pint			
2 cups	= 1 pint		
2 pints	= 1 quart		
4 quarts (liquid) = 1 gallon			
1 litre = approximately 4 cups or 1 quart			

Temprature conversion

Description	C° (CELSIUS)	=F° (FAHRENHEIT)	= GAS MARK
Very slow	120	= 250	= 1
Slow	150	= 300	= 2
Moderately slow	160	= 325	= 3
Moderate	180	= 350	= 4
Moderately hot	190	= 375	= 5
Hot	200	= 400	= 6
Very hot	230	= 450	=7

"Potjie" for two

Spice substations

Allspice	Cinnamon; cassia; dash of nutmeg or mace; or dash of cloves
Aniseed	Fennel seed or a few drops anise extract
Cardamom	Ginger
Chili Powder	Dash bottled hot pepper sauce plus a combination of oregano and cumin
Cinnamon	Nutmeg or allspice (use only 1/4 of the amount)
Cloves	Allspice; cinnamon; or nutmeg
Cumin	Chili powder
Ginger	Allspice; cinnamon; mace; or nutmeg
Mace	Allspice; cinnamon; ginger; or nutmeg
Mustard (dry or ground)	Wasabi powder (1/4 to 1/2 as much since it is hotter); horseradish powder; 1 teaspoon dry mustard powder = 1 Tablespoon prepared mustard
Nutmeg	Cinnamon; ginger; or mace
Saffron	Dash turmeric or annato powder (for color)
Turmeric	Dash saffron (for color) plus ground mustard powder (one to one ratio); annato powder

Herb Substitutions

Basil	Oregano or thyme
Chervil	Tarragon or parsley
Chives	Green onions (scallions); onion; or leek
Cilantro	Parsley
Italian Seasoning	Blend of any of these: basil, oregano, rosemary, and ground red pepper
Marjoram	Basil; thyme; or savory
Mint	Basil; marjoram; or rosemary
Oregano	Thyme or basil
Parsley	Chervil or cilantro
Poultry Seasoning	Sage plus a blend of any of these: thyme, marjoram, savory, black pepper, and rosemary
Red Pepper Flakes (dried chiles)	Dash bottled hot pepper sauce or black pepper
Rosemary	Thyme; tarragon; or savory
Sage	Poultry seasoning; savory; marjoram; or rosemary
Savory	Thyme; marjoram; or sage
Tarragon	Chervil; dash fennel seed; or dash aniseed
Thyme	Basil; marjoram; oregano; or savory

SIMPLE STARTERS

Cheese Bites

Prep Time:10 minutes
Cook Time:10 minutes
Surprisingly simple warm snacks to accompany a pre-dinner drinks

Ingredients(Makes 24)
1 tub plain Feta Cheese (200 g nett)
140 g chilli-bite mix powder (225 ml)
  Sweet Chilli Sauce

Method
Cut each feta round equally into 8 wedges.
Mix enough water into the chilli bite mix, to make a soft dropping consistency.
Gently heat a pan of sunflower oil to a depth of 3 cm.
Turn each feta wedge in the chilli bite batter until completely but not too thickly coated, and transfer directly into the hot oil. Fry for 15-20 seconds, turning over once, until the coating is puffy and lightly browned all over. Using a slotted spoon, lift out the bites onto crumpled kitchen paper to drain slightly.
Serve freshly fried with a dipping bowl of Sweet Chilli sauce.

Hints and Tips
For cocktail parties and bulk catering, supply a bowl of toothpicks or cocktail wooden forks for purposes of food hygiene when dipping.

BAKED CAMEMBERT WITH FIGS AND HONEY

Prep Time:5 minutes
Cook Time:5-10 minutes

A delicious, melt in the mouth starter that's easy to prepare in the oven or over coals.

Ingredients(4)
1 Camembert
1tsp Honey
2 sprigs of thyme or marjoram
* 2 fresh or preserved figs
1 large square of foil
* Preserved watermelon, fresh grapes or berries can be used as an alternative.

Method
Place the Camembert in the middle of the foil square.
Cut figs into eighths and place on top of cheese. Drizzle with honey and add herbs.
Wrap foil parcel by folding each corner into the middle and twisting into an easy carry parcel.
Oven: Place in a preheated oven at 180°c for 5 - 10 minutes.

Braai: Place next to the coals or on grid for 5 - 10 minutes. Do not heat for too long as cheese will become too runny.

BULLS EYE SAVOURIES

Prep Time:20 minutes
Cook Time:15 minutes
An excellent fool proof recipe for those pre-dinner savories.

Ingredients(Yields 24)
120 g   cake flour (250 ml)
125 g   butter or margarine
125 g   cheddar cheese, grated (250 ml)
1 pouch pitted green olives
6 peppadews (baby sweet peppers), quartered

Method
Pre-heat oven to 180 ° C. Lightly coat a large baking tray with baking spray.
Tip the olives into a sieve, and set aside over a bowl, for the brine to drain off thoroughly.
Squeeze a slice of peppadew® through the wider hole of each olive, to completely fill each centre.
Combine the flour, butter and cheese by hand, or in a food processor, to obtain a smooth ball of dough.
Pinch off small amounts of pastry and enclose a stuffed olive in it, rolling gently on the worktop to achieve a ball the size of a large marble.
Bake the balls spaced apart, on the prepared baking tray, in the pre-heated oven for 15 minutes.
Lift using an egg lifter after a few minutes of cooling.
Serve warm or at room temperature.

Hints and Tips
Swop the peppadew for finely shredded biltong when stuffing the olives, to add a meaty flavor twist surprise.
If using your hands to rub the dough ingredients together, grate the cold butter or margarine block directly onto the flour, using a cheese grater. The rubbing in process is so much easier then.
Do not roll the dough layer around the olive too thickly, or it will not bake through well.

SPARE-RIB SALAD

Prep Time:15 minutes
Cook Time:10 minutes
A filling salad bursting with the summer flavors of pineapple, avocado and mint.

Ingredients(Serves: 4)

1 small pineapple, peeled and cubed
100 ml fresh mint, chopped
1 Ripe and Ready avocado pear, cubed
1 tray sugar-snap peas (125 g)
500 g box   pork-rib burgers

Method

Preheat the oven grill with the oven-shelf one above centre position.
Lightly combine the pineapple, mint and avocado pear cubes and chill.
Briefly cook the peas in the microwave oven for 2 minutes, with 20 ml water.
Refresh in cold water, drain, and add to the salad ingredients.
Grill the ribs in an oven dish for 8 - 10 minutes, basting with the marinade.
Using kitchen scissors, snip into even strips.
Lightly toss into the chilled salad ingredients and serve immediately.

Hints and Tips
There is no need for salad dressing as the marinade and fruit
provide sufficient moisture and flavour.
Recommended accompaniment: crusty bread loaf or monastery bread rolls
Recommended wine: Rhine Riesling or light pinotage

STUFFED MUSHROOMS

Prep Time:10 minutes
Cook Time:5 minutes
A delicious vegetarian starter where the flavours of brown mushroom, chilli, garlic and cheese fuse into a treat for your palate.

Ingredients(Serves: 4)

8 flat brown mushrooms, cleaned
4 slices oat & honey low GI bread
1 jar   chilli and garlic salsa
1 large Granny Smith apple, peeled and grated
100 g   mild chilli cheese, grated

Method
 Lightly drizzle a little olive oil over each cleaned mushroom, and place them in rows in a baking dish.
Pre-heat the oven on GRILL setting.
Crumble the bread into a bowl, and combine with the salsa and apple.
Generously pile the mixture onto each mushroom cap.
Top with grated cheese and place the baking dish in the pre-heated oven until the cheese is melted and the mushrooms tender. Serve immediately.

Hints and Tips
Remember to peel off the thick wax layer from the cheese before grating!
Recommended wine: Semi sweet white wine

THE MAIN`S
BEEF AND BEER POT

Ingredients (Serves 1, # ¼ pot)

15ml Cake flour 5ml Paprika
300g Beef fillet, cubed 15ml Butter
15ml Oil
1 Medium onions, thinly sliced 15ml White sugar
10 Green beans, cut up
3 Carrots, peeled and thinly sliced
1 Garlic clove, chopped 15ml Mixed herbs 375ml Beer
125ml Beef stock
1 Packet tomato soup powder
1 Bay leaf 15ml Vinegar
10ml Maizena (corn flour) Salt and pepper to taste

Method

1.Coat the meat with a mixture of the flour and paprika. Heat the oil and butter in the pot and brown the meat.
2.Remove the meat and brown the onions, garlic and sugar until the onions is nice and soft.
3.Replace the meat and stir in the herbs, beer, beef stock, soup powder and bay leaf. Cover with the lid and allow the pot to simmer for a 1 hour or until the meat is tender.
4.Add the beans and carrots, cover with the lid and allow the pot to simmer for about 30 minutes.

Beef and Vegetable Pot

Ingredients (Serves 1, # ¼ pot)

10ml Cooking oil
300g Stewing beef, cubed 1 Medium onions, sliced
50 ml Dried apricots, soaked in water for 1 hour before 4 Carrots, peeled and sliced
1 Medium sweet potatoes, peeled and sliced
1 Medium potatoes, peeled and sliced
3 Baby marrows, sliced 75ml Cabbage, chopped 1 Tomato, peeled and sliced
Black pepper to taste
15ml Dried parsley

Sauce

100ml Sweet Sherry/Port 25ml Soya sauce
5ml Black pepper 3ml Dry mustard 1ml Dry rosemary 1ml Dry thyme
1/4 Cube beef stock ml Boiling water

Method

1.Heat the oil in the pot and brown the meat and kidney till almost brown.
Add the onions and brown together.
2.Mix the ingredients of the sauce and add it to the pot. Stir well, cover with
the lid and simmer for 1 hour.
3.Layer the dried fruit and then the veggies as they appear in the recipe.
Sprinkle some pepper over the tomatoes.
4.Cover with the lid and allow the pot to simmer for about 1 hour or until the
veggies are done.

OXTAIL AND BANANA POT

Ingredients (serves 1, # ¼ pot)

¼ of Large oxtail, cut into pieces
1 Medium onions, finely sliced
1 Ripe bananas, sliced
2 Medium carrots, cut into strips
3 Baby potatoes
50g Button mushrooms
½ medium tomato, sliced 5ml Chopped parsley
1 Garlic cloves, finely chopped 30ml Butter
¼ Red chilli, finely chopped
2 Whole cloves (kruinaeltjies) 5ml Mixed herbs
1 Bay leaves 250ml Warm water
Salt and pepper to taste

The sauce

30ml Brown vinegar
10ml Tomato sauce,
10ml Chutney
10ml Honey
5ml Medium curry powder

Method

1.Coat the Pot with the butter and heat.
2.Braai the meat for about 15 minutes.
3.Add the onions, garlic, chilli, cloves, herbs, bay leaves, salt and pepper and braai for a further 15 minutes.(If the Pot gets too dry, add some warm water)
4.Add the 250ml warm water, cover with the lid and allow the Potjie to simmer for about 30 minutes.
5.In the meantime, mix the ingredients of the sauce and put one side.
6.After 30 minutes, pack the bananas on top of the meat and layer the vegetables as they appear in the recipe
7.Sprinkle the parsley on top, and then layer the onions and allow the Potjie to simmer for ½ hour
8.Add the sauce and allow to simmer for a further 30 minutes.

OXTAIL POT

Ingredients (serves 1, # ¼ pot)

500g Oxtails cut 2 inches thick pieces
10 slices Bacon cut in 1 inch pieces
½ cup Flour seasoned with salt and pepper 1 litre beef stock
1 can tomato paste
1 Bay leaf
6 black peppercorns
1 bouquet garni
6 large leeks, chopped coarsely
2 large onions, chopped coarsely
6 large carrots, chopped coarsely
20 button mushrooms
1 cup red wine
½   cup sherry
½   cup cream
2 tablespoons butter
2 tablespoons olive oil
2 tablespoons crushed garlic

Method

1.   Dry oxtails with paper towel. Put seasoned flour in a Ziplock bag, then add the Oxtail and shake to coat with flour.
2.   Heat butter and olive oil and saute bacon pieces. Remove bacon and brown Oxtail in resulting fat, remove and drain.
3.   Finely dice 4 of the carrots. Coarsely chop the onions and the leeks.
4.   Add the finely diced carrots, leeks, onions and saute until softened
5.   Add Oxtail, bacon, bouquet garni, bay leaf, peppercorns, garlic, tomato sauce, red wine, sherry.
6.   Bring slowly to a boil and cook slowly for 3 - 4 hours.
7.   1 Hour before serving cut the remaining carrots into 1 inch pieces, add them and mushrooms and continue cooking slowly.
8.   Just prior to serving, add cream and stir in.
9.   If you want to thicken the sauce mix some cornstarch with the cream before adding.

MUTTON-COMBINATION POT

Ingredients (serves 1, # ¼ pot)

30ml Butter
300g mixed meat, i.e. Shanks, Rib, Neck ,1Medium-sized onions, diced
5 Baby potatoes, peeled 100g Frozen mixed vegetables
1 Medium sized sweet potatoes, sliced Salt and pepper to taste

Sauce

250ml Warm water
½ Cubes of beef stock 125ml Dry red wine 50ml Chutney
20ml Tomato sauce 30ml Worcester sauce 25ml Soya sauce
30ml Maizena (corn flour) 30ml Oxtail soup powder 15ml Bisto
10ml Garlic crushed
0.6ml Fine clove (kruienaeltjies)

This delicious pot is best served with yellow rice and raisins.

Method

1.Heat the pot until it is very hot add the butter. Then brown a few pieces of meat at a time and remove.
2.Brown the onions in the meat's fat until soft.
3.Return the meat to the pot and layer the potatoes and sweet potatoes on top of the meat.
4.Mix all the ingredients of the sauce and pour over the food in the pot. Add salt and pepper to taste.
5.Finally, cover with the lid and allow to simmer for approximately 3 hours (add the mixed veggies after 1 hour).

LAMB SHANKS & VEGETABLE POT

Ingredients (serves 1, # ¼ pot)

30ml Butter
12 Pieces lamb shanks
4 Medium-size onions, diced 240ml Water
6 black pepper corns
4 Bay leaves
3 Whole cloves (clove (kruienaeltjies) 15ml Salt
15ml Aromat 10ml Dried parsley
2.5ml Ground black pepper 500g Baby carrots, peeled
12 Medium potatoes, quartered
500g Cauliflower
500g Whole button mushrooms
6 Baby marrow, sliced
4 Tomatoes, cubed
500g Mixed dried fruit, soaked in water 1 hour
250ml Dry white wine 90ml Bisto in 125ml water

Method
1.Heat the pot and melt the butter. Then brown a few pieces of meat at a time and remove.
2.Brown the onions until soft.
3.Return the meat and add the water, pepper-corns, bay leaves and 'whole cloves' and 10ml of the salt.
4.Cover with the lid and allow the pot to simmer for about 1 hour.
5.Mix the aromat, parsley, pepper and the remaining salt and sprinkle in-between the layered vegetables (layer the veggies as they appear in the recipe).
6.Place the dried fruit on top and allow the pot to simmer for about 1.5 hours.
7.Sprinkle a little aromat over the pot, cover with the lid and allow to simmer for 30 minutes.
8.Finally, add the wine and the bisto solution 30 minutes before the pot is served.

WATERBLOMMETJIE POT

Ingredients (serves 1, # ¼ pot)
250g Waterblommetjies 4 Pieces of lamb shank
1Medium-size onions, diced 150ml Water
6 Black pepper corns
4 Bay leaves
3 Whole clove (kruienaeltjies) 15ml Salt
15ml Aromat 10ml Dried parsley
2.5ml Ground black pepper 125g Baby carrots, peeled 3 Small potatoes,
halved 125g Cauliflower
125g Whole button mushrooms
6 Baby marrow, sliced
 4 Tomatoes, cubed
125g Mixed dried fruit, soaked in water for 1 hour
125ml Dry white wine
90ml Bisto in 125ml water

Method

1.Heat the pot and melt the butter. Then brown a few pieces of meat at a time
and remove.
2.Brown the onions until soft.
3.Return the meat and add the water, pepper-corns, bay leaves and 'whole
cloves' and 10ml of the salt.
4.Cover with the lid and allow the pot to simmer for about 30 minutes.
5.Mix the aromat, parsley, pepper and the remaining salt and sprinkle in-
between the layered vegetables (layer the veggies as they appear in the recipe).
6.Place the dried fruit on top and allow the pot to simmer for about 30
minutes.
7.Sprinkle a little aromat over the pot, cover with the lid and allow to simmer
for 30 minutes.
8.Finally, add the wine and the bisto solution 30 minutes before the pot is
served.

EASY CHICKEN POT

Ingredients

45 ml cooking oil
250g chicken thighs
10 ml salt
4 bay leaves pinch dried thyme
4 black pepper corns pinch ground allspice 45 ml chutney
125 ml carrots, peeled and sliced
6 large potatoes, peeled and sliced
125 g whole button mushrooms
125 ml boiling water
¼ chicken stock cube

Method

1.Heat the oil in the pot.
2.Sprinkle the thighs with salt and fry the chicken, a few pieces at a time, until golden brown.
3.Add the herbs, spices and chutney.
4.Arrange the carrots, potatoes and mushrooms in layers on top of the chicken.
5.Dissolve the stock cube in the water and add it to the potjie.
6.Replace the lid and simmer for approximately 1 hour and 20 minutes. Add water if the potjie becomes too dry.

CHICKEN CURRY POT

Ingredients (serves 1, # ¼ pot)

1 table spoon sunflower oil
1 medium onions, finely chopped
2 garlic cloves, finely chopped
1 table spoon mild to strong curry powder
1 chicken pieces {the breast works best} Salt to taste
4 potatoes, peeled and cut into pieces
1 cup of rice
¼ cup brown lentils, soaked (optional)
1 cup of water
½ can (400g) finely chopped tomato
½ can (400g) coconut milk

Method

1.Heat the oil and fry the onion and garlic until soft. Add the curry powder and fr y for 1 minute.
2.Fry chicken pieces in onion mixture until brown.
3.Add the rest of the ingredients, close with lid tightly secure. Over medium coals let your potjie simmer for an hour to hour-and 30 minutes.

Remember the chutney.

Salad

Finely chop tomato, onion and cucumber and mix it in a bowl with little vinegar and a teaspoon of sugar. Serve with curry.

CHICKEN AND NOODLE POT

Ingredients (serves 1, # ¼ pot)

2 Chicken breasts
Salt and pepper to taste 30ml Cooking oil
1 Celery sticks, chopped
1 Tomatoes sliced
1 Green pepper, cut lengthwise
250g Whole button mushrooms 250ml Spring onion, chopped 15ml Parsley,
finely chopped 10ml Mixed herbs
250ml Uncooked shell noodles 5ml Ground black pepper 3ml Dried rosemary
200ml Dry white wine
250ml Grated cheddar cheese

Method

1.Spice the chicken with the salt and pepper.
2.Heat the oil in the pot and braai the chicken, a few pieces at a time, until
golden brown.
3.Layer the vegetables in the order as above and sprinkle the parsley and
mixed herbs over all.
4.Now add the shell noodles and sprinkle the pepper and rosemary over
before pouring the wine over all the ingredients.
5.Cover with the lid and allow to simmer for about 1 hour.
6.Sprinkle the cheese over and allow to simmer for a final 20 minutes.

CHICKEN - BILTONG & BACON POT

Ingredients (serves 1, # ¼ pot)

1/2 blocks of chicken stock 125ml Boiling water 200ml white wine
250ml Chutney
46g Mushroom soup powder (1 packet) 5ml Dried thyme
5ml Mixed herbs 5ml Lemon pepper 15ml Olive oil
15ml Butter
2 Chicken pieces (breast)
150g Bacon, chopped 50ml Brandy
10ml Garlic chopped 2 Onions, cut into rings
½ Green pepper , roughly chopped 1 Celery stick, cut into thin rings
5 Small potatoes, peeled
 1 Carrots, cut into discs
2 Small onions, whole
125g Button mushrooms
8 Marrow mix, cut in thick slices
1 Red pepper, cut into long strips
150g Wet beef biltong, carved
100ml Grated cheese
125 ml Fresh parsley, chopped

Dissolve the stock cubes in boiling water. Mix all the sauce ingredients and add to stock mixture. Keep one side.

Method

1. Heat butter and oil over medium heat and brown the chicken.
2. Add the bacon and fry for 3 minutes.
3. Add the brandy and garlic and mix well, then do not stir again.
4. Sort the onion, green pepper and celery over the chicken and place the potatoes and carrots on top.
5. Pour over the sauce, place the lid on and simmer for 1 hour.
6. Add the onion, mushroom, marrow and red pepper, and finish with biltong and cheese.
7. Add boiling water if needed, close lid and simmer for a further 20 min.
8. Stir just before serving and finally add parsley.

BILTONG POT

Ingredients (serves 1, # ¼ pot)

500g Biltong, cut
500g Pasta (any form, except spaghetti)
250g Butter or Margarine
½ Onion, chopped
¼ Packet, diced mushrooms
1 Table spoon crushed garlic
½ packets instant white sauce / cream of mushroom soup Hand full of
mixed fresh herbs
250ml Cream
150ml grated cheese

Method

1.Melt the butter, fry onion, garlic and mushroom.
2.Take some coals out if you have to, your pot must now be cooked on low
heat. Add the biltong.
3.Add the pasta, mix the packets of instant sauce with enough water to ensure
it covers everything.
4.Add the herbs then close the lid, just check now and again that there is
enough water.
5.Once paste is cooked, take pot of the coals, add cream and cheese and mix
well.

PORK FILLET POT

Ingredients (serves 1, # ¼ pot)

1 Pork fillets, approx 300g each
5 Large seedless prunes
5 Smoked oysters 20ml Butter
20ml Cooking oil 15ml Cake flour
200ml - 250ml Beef stock 125ml Red wine
Salt to taste
5ml Black pepper 12 Baby onions
5 Celery sticks, sliced
4 Baby potatoes, peeled 5ml Maizena
Freshly chopped parsley for garnish

Method

1.Cut a lengthwise groove in each fillet and open carefully. Fill 10 of the prunes with an oyster and arrange the filled prunes in the groove of one of the fillets. Cover with the other fillet and bind the two fillets tightly with a piece of string.
2.Heat the butter and oil and braai the meat until brown.
3.Sprinkle the cake flour over the fillets and brown for another 2 minutes.
4.Add the stock and the red wine and stir the sauce with a wooden spoon until smooth.
5.Season the meat with the salt and pepper and cover with the lid and allow the pot to simmer slowly for 1 hour.
6.Remove the string from the meat and cut in slices but keep the pieces against each other.
7.Pack the veggies around the meat in the pot, add the remaining prunes and add a little of the stock, if necessary, and allow the pot to simmer until the veggies are done.
8.Thicken the sauce with the maizena (mixed in a little water) if needed.
9.Garnish with the parsley before serving.

Roelof Beukes

SWEET AND SOUR POT

Ingredients (serves 1, # ¼ pot)

15ml Butter
1 medium onions, sliced
¼ Green pepper, sliced 500g Leg of pork, cubed 10ml Finely mixed spices
Salt and pepper to taste
¼ Large pineapple, peeled and sliced
¼ Large cooking apple, peeled and sliced 125ml Brown vinegar
60ml Maizena 60ml Brown sugar 60ml Red wine
25ml Worcester sauce 250ml Boiling water

Method

1.Melt the butter in the pot and brown the onions and green peppers until soft.
2.Remove and brown the meat.
3.Sprinkle the spices, salt and pepper over the meat.
4.Cover with the lid and allow the pot to simmer for approximately 1 hour.
5.Place the pineapple on top of the meat, then the apple and then the onion and green pepper mix. Simmer for a further 1 hour.
6.Mix the rest of the ingredients and pour over the pot.

OSTRICH POT

Ingredients (serves 1, # ¼ pot)

30ml Cooking oil
375g Ostrich neck slices 4 Leeks, sliced
2 Fat cloves garlic, crushed
5ml Dried or 1 sprig fresh rosemary 100g Brown mushrooms, sliced
30ml Boiled green peppercorns, bruised 75ml Brandy
50ml Dry sherry
375ml Dry red wine or ½ red wine ½ chicken stock 30ml Lemon juice
15 Fresh pickling onions, peeled
5 Small whole carrots
4 Small, peeled potatoes or un-peeled new potatoes scrubbed clean
1 x 100 g packet creamed spinach and mushrooms, thawed. (Can be replaced
with 250 g cooked, chopped and flavored spinach mixed with 125 ml sour
cream. Flavor the spinach with some of the following: bacon, ham, cheese,
nutmeg and lemon juice)
15ml Cake flour
Little milk
Pinch nutmeg
Salt to taste

Method

1.Heat the oil in the pot and brown the meat a little at a time. Remove and set
aside.
2.Fry the leeks, garlic, rosemary, mushrooms and peppercorns in the same
pot.
3.Return the meat to the pot. Heat the brandy slightly, pour over the meat,
and ignite. Add the heated sherry, red wine and lemon juice once the flames
have died down. Cover with the lid, reduce the heat and simmer for 1 hour or
till the meat is almost tender.
4.Layer the vegetables, except the spinach, on top of the meat, cover, and
simmer for a further 45 to 50 minutes.
5.Mix the spinach mixture with a paste of cake flour and milk and spoon
carefully over the food in the pot.
6.Season with nutmeg and salt, cover and simmer for a further 15 minutes.

VENISON POT (WILDSPOTJIE)

Ingredients (serves 1, # ¼ pot)

125ml Sunflower oil
4 Medium carrots, sliced
2 Medium onions, sliced
2 Cloves garlic, crushed 10ml Chopped fresh thyme 1kg Venison, cubed
250g Rind-less bacon, chopped 500ml Port or dry red wine
6 Medium potatoes, sliced

Method

1.Heat the oil in a pot and saute the carrots, onions and garlic for about 5 minutes.
2.Add the thyme, meat, bacon and port and simmer, covered, for 1 hour.
3.Add the potatoes and simmer for a further 35 minutes to a hour.

PAELLA POT

Ingredients (serves 1, # ¼ pot)

60 ml Cooking oil
3 Red sweet peppers (seeded and cut in strips) or a 400g tin pimento 1
medium onion, chopped
250g Pork, cubed
1 Chicken thighs, halved
300ml boiling water
5 ml saffron
4 Bay leaves
½ Chicken stock cubes
1 kg Kingklip fillets, cut in strips
100g Frozen prawns
125g Uncooked rice Salt and pepper to taste 75g Frozen green peas Juice of 1
lemon

Method

1.Heat the oil in the pot. Lightly brown the pepper, onion, pork and chicken.
2.Cover and simmer slowly for a hour or until the meat is nearly done.
3.Add the saffron, bay leaves and chicken stock cubes to the boiling water and
set aside.
4.Place the fish and prawns on top of the meat, followed by the rice and peas.
5.Season with salt and pepper to taste. Add the saffron water little by little as
the rice boils dry.
6.Simmer the potjie gently until the rice and peas are done and all the liquid
has nearly boiled away.

Paella should be loose and the rice should not be soggy. Simmer slowly to
prevent rice from burning.
Add the lemon juice just before serving and stir well.

CRAYFISH POT

Ingredients (serves 1, # ¼ pot)

45ml Cooking oil 750ml Uncooked rice
1 Medium onion, chopped
1.5L Water
10ml Dried parsley
1 Garlic clove, crushed Juice of Lemon
150g Sliced mushroom
2 Tomatoes, peeled and diced
1 Packet white onion soup
2 Uncooked crayfish tails Salt to taste

Method

1.Allow the parsley to soak in the water for 15 minutes.
2.Heat the oil in the pot, add the onions, garlic and peppers and brown until soft.
3.Add the parsley water and rice, cook for a 10 minutes.
4.Add the rest of the ingredients except the crayfish.
5.Sprinkle the salt over and cover with the lid. Allow the pot to simmer slowly for 30 minutes or until the rice is almost done.
6.Now place the crayfish tails on top of the pot and allow it to simmer for 15 minutes.

Don't cook the crayfish for too long as it could get soggy.

SIDE DISHES

RICE IN THE POTJIE

Potjie No: ½
Serves: 2 as a side dish
Cooking Time: 1 hour
Print Recipe » Email Recipe »
Ingredients
200 g Rice
1 large onion, chopped
15 ml butter
15 ml cooking oil
500ml water
5 ml salt

Method
Heat butter and oil in larger potjie.
Add onion and sauté until tran ent.
Add Barely and stir until it is coated with oil.
Heat water and salt to boiling point in smaller potjie
Cover with lid and simmer slowly for 40-45 minutes or until Barely is cooked.
Add more boiling water if necessary.
Do not stir during cooking process.
If desired, stir in a large knob of butter just before serving.

BARELY IN THE POTJIE

Potjie No: ½
Serves: 2 as a side dish
Cooking Time: 1 hour
Print Recipe » Email Recipe »
Ingredients
200 g Barely
1 large onion, chopped
15 ml butter
15 ml cooking oil
500ml water
2 ml salt

Method
Heat butter and oil in larger potjie.
Add onion and sauté until tran ent.
Add Barely and stir until it is coated with oil.
Heat water and salt to boiling point in smaller potjie
Cover with lid and simmer slowly for 40-45 minutes or until Barely is cooked.
Add more boiling water if necessary.
Do not stir during cooking process.
If desired, stir in a large knob of butter just before serving.

DESSERTS

BANANA LOLLY

Prep Time:10 minutes
Cook Time:1 hr to freeze
This is a fun way to end the night of and this sweet treat a healthier choice than the normal dessert options.

Ingredients(1)
1 small ripe firm banana, peeled
  smooth peanut butter
Chopped peanuts or toasted coconut or or oat-cluster cereal with chocolate chips
Wooden skewers

Method
Push a wooden skewer through the centre length of the banana to near the end.
Spread a light coating of peanut butter all over the banana.
Holding the banana by its skewer, roll it in your choice of coating, pressing lightly until well covered.
Freeze for at least 1 hour.

Hints and Tips
To toast coconut, shake the coconut in a dry frying pan, over medium heat until golden in colour. Use it when completely cooled.
Do not swop this cereal for a granola with raisins, as they freeze too hard for easy eating.

HONEY CARAMEL ORANGES

Prep Time:10 minutes
Cook Time:20 minutes
Orange slices drenched in a honey and cinnamon glaze. A zesty, healthy dessert option to end the ocation.

Ingredients(Serves 5)
5 large oranges
1 ml caramel or vanilla essence
50 g light brown sugar
30 ml honey
100 ml water
2 cinnamon sticks

Method
Using a zester, peel off thin shreds from the skin of one of the oranges.
Peel all the oranges carefully, ensuring that all the white pith is removed too.
Slice the oranges across the width, into 6 slices each.
Arrange the slices in a shallow heat-proof dish.
In a heavy based saucepan, combine the essence, sugar, honey and water. Stir over medium heat to dissolve the sugar. Once the mixture boils, add in the orange rind and cinnamon. Simmer briskly for 5 minutes, without stirring, to a light golden colour.
Pour over the orange slices. Serve warm or cold.

Hints and Tips
For a special touch for entertaining, stir in 25 ml whisky to the honey syrup before pouring onto the sliced oranges. If you do not have a zester tool, step 1 is optional.
Serve with vanilla ice cream or 175 ml thick Double Cream Plain Yoghurt as is, or combined with 15 ml lemon curd.
Sprinkle a crumbled ginger-nut biscuit or fudge square over each serving.

QUICK APPLE PIE

Prep Time:15 minutes
Cook Time:35 minutes
Feel like a warm apple pie but can't be bothered to make pastry? This apple sponge pudding is filled with sweet apple goodness and can be served the same way.
Find Other Recipes

Browse Categories

Ingredients(Serves: 8)
3 large eggs
1 can condensed milk
315 ml cake flour (150 g)
5 ml ground cinnamon
5 ml vanilla essence
30 ml soft margarine
10 ml baking powder
410 g can pie apples, chopped
* smooth apricot jam for glaze

Method
1. Preheat oven to 180 ° C. Grease a Good Living 679 ml Oval Stoneware dish, or similar.
2. In a 1.5 litre Good Living porcelain mixing bowl, whisk together the eggs until fluffy and doubled in volume.
3. Beat in the condensed milk. Gently blend in the remaining ingredients.
4. Pour the batter into the prepared dish.
5. Bake for 35 minutes.
6. Brush over a little warmed smooth apricot jam.
Hints and Tips
Substitute the apples for canned pears pieces

MOCHA PEDRO

Prep Time:10 minutes
Give the traditional Dom Pedro a fun coffee- twist with the help of convenient cappuccino sachets. Wonderfully quick for a dessert when entertaining!
Find Other Recipes

Browse Categories

Ingredients(5)
2 litre   Caramel &Vanilla flavoured ice cream (1 tub)
5 sachets   Café Express Cappuccino (6 sachets)
125 ml boiling water
125 ml whisky (5 tot-measures)

Method
Break up the ice cream in its tub, and tip the contents into a food processor bowl.
Cut open the cappuccino sachets and pour their contents into a jug. Pour on the boiling water and stir until dissolved. Stir in the whisky.
Pour this warm liquid over the ice cream, and process until evenly blended and smooth.
Pour into 6 tumblers, and serve a wide-mouthed straw with each.
Hints and Tips
Plain vanilla ice cream can also be used.

CHOCOLATE VOLCANO LAVA PUDDING

Prep Time:15 minutes
Cook Time:20 minutes
Bring out the chef in you with this warm gooey chocolate pudding that's easy but impressive!
Find Other Recipes

Browse Categories

Ingredients(12)
Melted butter, for greasing
Cocoa powder for dusting
275g dark chocolate
225g butter
400g castor sugar
1 Vanilla Pod or 3 ml Vanilla essence
5 eggs, beaten
200g Cake Wheat flour, sifted
Method
Heat the oven to 180 C. Brush 12 dariole pudding moulds or ramekins with melted butter, dust with cocoa powder and shake out the excess. Set aside.
Melt the chocolate and butter gently in a saucepan. Remove from the heat and stir in the sugar and vanilla seeds scraped off the pod or vanilla essence. Leave to cool slightly.
Beat the eggs into the mixture a little at a time, and then fold in the sifted flour and a little salt until you have a smooth mixture.
Divide between the moulds – each one two thirds full. Place on the middle shelf of the oven and cook for 18 -20 minutes until firm but still wobbly.
Remove from the oven, run a knife round the edges, invert and tip out on to serving plates. Serve immediately with vanilla ice cream.

Hints and Tips
This dessert is also delicious served with fresh fruit. Slice a few Freshline Strawberries, Kiwis and dot with blueberries.

Roelof Beukes

Printed in Great Britain
by Amazon